Ayn Rand
and
Contemporary
Business Ethics

Our Mission

The Atlas Society's mission is to inspire people to embrace reason, achievement, benevolence and ethical self-interest as the moral foundation for political liberty, personal happiness and a flourishing society.

We build on Ayn Rand's works and ideas, and use artistic and other creative means to reach and inspire new audiences. We promote an open and empowering brand of Objectivism; we welcome engagement with all who honestly seek to understand the philosophy, and we use reason, facts and open debate in the search for truth above all else; we do not appeal to authority or conflate personalities with ideas. We resist moral judgment without adequate facts, and believe disagreement does not necessarily imply evasion.

Ayn Rand and Contemporary Business Ethics

Stephen R.C. Hicks, Ph.D.

The Atlas Society Press

"This essay by The Atlas Society Senior Scholar Stephen Hicks is a justification of capitalism and of Ayn Rand's ethics of egoism in business. It was originally published in the *Journal of Accounting, Ethics, & Public Policy* in 2003. Fifteen years later, Hicks's arguments remain important. Today, sundry politicians and activists cynically perpetuate the myths of Socialism by targeting profitable businesses with regulations and fines in the name of the environment and the needy. Bureaucrats attempt to usurp credit for the accomplishments of Capitalism by claiming, 'Nobody in this country got rich on their own.' Hicks makes the case that Ayn Rand's moral defense of individualism and Capitalism remains the best refutation of the anti-business agenda."

— Marilyn Moore, Contributing Editor, The Atlas Society.

Published by
The Atlas Society Press
22001 Northpark Drive, Suite 250
Kingwood TX 77339

Library of Congress Cataloging-in-Publication Data:
   Hicks, Stephen R.C., 1960—
   Ayn Rand and Contemporary Business Ethics/Stephen R. C.
      Hicks
   ISBN 978-1-7326037-2-1

Printed in the United States of America

Cover design by Matthew Holdridge

Contents

Ayn Rand and Contemporary Business Ethics

Introduction: Business and the Free Society

Advocates of the free society think of business as an integral part of the dynamic, progressive society they advocate. In the West, the rise of a culture hospitable to business has unleashed incalculable productive energies. Business professionals have taken the products of science and revolutionized the fields of agriculture, transportation, and medicine. Business professionals have taken the products of art and dramatically increased our access to them. We have more food, we are more mobile, we have more health care, we have more access to works of fiction, theater, and music than anyone could reasonably have predicted a few centuries ago.

The result of business in the West, and more recently in parts of the East, has been an enormous rise in the standard of human living. We have gone, in the space of a few centuries, from a time in which perhaps 10% of the population lived comfortably while 90% lived near subsistence to a time in which 90% live better than comfortably and 10% live near subsistence. And we haven't given up on the remaining 10%.

Intellectuals who study the free society have, in the fields of economics and politics, a good understanding of what makes this possible: individualism. In economics there exists a well worked out understanding of how, starting with autonomous individuals engaging in voluntary transactions, goods, services, and information flow efficiently to where they are needed. In politics there exists a good understanding of how protecting individual rights and limiting government power prevent the arbitrariness and stultification that suppress individuals' creativity and incentive in all areas of life. This is not to say that individualist theories in economics and politics have carried the day; but they have had a major impact, they have had and continue to have many able advocates, and even their opponents give them a respectful hearing.

The same is not true, however, for individualism in ethics. Individualism in ethics is the thesis of egoism: the view that the individual is the standard of value, that individuals are ends in themselves. But traditional ethics has always found egoism to be highly problematic. So it has always found large-scale and consistent expressions of egoism problematic—such as those in the business world. The business world is a network of individuals, each with his own agenda in life, each working primarily for his own profit, and each interacting with others only if it is to his benefit. Business is a social world governed by self- interest, and moral evaluations of self-interest that determine moral evaluations of the business world.

My purpose in this essay is to defend the egoism that the business world depends upon. Business is about production and trade. Production is a consequence of individuals' taking responsibility for their lives and exercising rational judgment about their needs and how to fulfill them. Trade is a consequence of productive individuals' willingness to interact cooperatively to mutual benefit. These principles—responsibility, rationality, cooperation—are core principles in any healthy moral system and form the core principles of the business world.

Of course not all individuals in the business world act responsibly, rationally, and cooperatively. Such problem cases are, however, aberrations. Business exists and flourishes to the extent individuals in the business world are productive and cooperative, so the major part of business ethics should be about what principles enable individuals to function productively and cooperatively. But because of the problems that can be created by irresponsible, irrational, and uncooperative individuals, part of business ethics deals with how productive individuals should solve the problems caused by the irresponsible.

This thesis, however, implies a recasting of current business ethics, since the currently dominant models hold the reverse—that business is, in principle, amoral or immoral, and that ethical behavior is the exception.

My thesis is that the core of business is moral just as the core of any valid profession is moral: education, science, art. The profession of education creates value: the transmission of knowledge from one generation to the next. The profession of science creates value: the discovery of new knowledge. The profession of art creates value: objects that express and evoke important human themes. In each profession, some individuals act unethically. But such individuals are quite rightly not taken as representative of the nature of education, science, art.

Business, however, is placed by most ethicists in a special, problematic category. In doing so, most contemporary business ethics does business a disservice. Worse than that, its proposed cures are plagued with intended and unintended consequences that are often much worse than the problems it is attempting to solve. So my task today is fourfold:

- To delineate the axioms of current business ethics—namely that self-interest and the profit motive are not moral, and that selflessness is required for ethical behavior.
- To probe the underlying ethical-theoretical considerations that lead to the rejection of self-interest and the promotion of selflessness—namely, that economics is a zero-sum game and that human nature is inherently destructive.
- To argue that a rational conception of self-interest solves the problems caused by taking human nature to be de-

structive or economics to be zero-sum—namely that humans are ends in themselves, that requirements of production are primary in ethics, and that reason applied to production eliminates the zero-sum scenario.

- To sketch what an ethic of rational self-interest implies for business ethics—namely, that all parties be seen as self-responsible agents who interact only to mutually agreed upon terms.

The Contemporary Literature: Business as Amoral or Immoral

In the current literature in business ethics, business is assumed to be at best an amoral enterprise, and the expectation is often that business practice is more likely than not to be immoral.

The reason for this is a nearly universally held thesis among business ethics: that moral considerations and the considerations that generally drive business are in completely different categories. Business is driven by self-interest and profit, but for all major business ethicists self-interest and profit are either amoral or immoral.

Alex Michalos, philosopher and editor-in-chief of the *Journal of Business Ethics,* writes: "Insofar as one is acting primarily in the interest of increasing profit, it is trivially true that one's primary interest is not in doing what is morally right."[1] Michalos' point is that it is not even arguable that profit-seeking and moral behavior are in different categories.

Two philosophically informed business professors write in *Academy of Management Review*: "Two normative views are common ... The first holds that, because executive level managers are agents for shareholders, maximizing the present value of the firm is the appropriate motivating principle for management. The second (e.g., normative stakeholder theory) holds that principled moral reasoning ought to motivate management decisions."[2] Here we contrast moral reasoning with maximizing the firm's owners' self-interest.

Amartya Sen, Harvard philosopher and economist, writes in a book on the relation between ethics and economics: "The self-interest view of rationality involves *inter alia* a firm rejection of the 'ethics-related' view of motivation."[3] Here we contrast self-interested motivation and ethical motivation.

Al Gini, co-author with leading business ethicist Tom Donaldson: "Doing the right thing because it's fashionable or in your own best interest doesn't ethically count—even if the desired results are achieved."[4] Here we read that ethics is not concerned with self-interest.

The list could be extended indefinitely. It is worth noting that the above quotations are taken from moderates in business ethics, i.e., from those who do not see themselves as in principle hostile to business or as wanting total government regulation of economic activity. The point is simply that the separation of ethics and self-interest is taken as axiomatic in current business ethics literature.

Participants in the literature then divide into two groups:

- Those who think morality and self-interest are in different categories—but do not think there is a general antagonism between the two.
- Those who think morality and self-interest are in different categories—and that there is a general antagonism between the two.

Members of the first group hold that the results of self-interested and moral consideration will sometimes conflict and sometimes coincide. The general purpose of business ethics, then, is to get businesses always to consider their actions from a moral in addition to a self-interested perspective and, if a conflict should arise, to be willing to sacrifice self-interest.

Members of the second group argue that morality is opposed to self-interest. For example, philosopher Norman Bowie writes: "The conscious pursuit of self-interest by all members of society has the collective result of undermining the interests of all."[5] Business ethicist Oliver Williams reports the conclusion of a conference on business ethics: "...there would be no facile resolution of the conflict between the values of a just society and the sharply opposing values of successful corporations."[6] William Shaw and Vincent Barry, authors of a widely-used business ethics textbook, write: "Morality serves to restrain our purely self-interested desires so we can all live together."[7] In each case, self-interest is the enemy—of justice, morality and the collective interest. Again, the list of quotations could be extended indefinitely.

For members of this second group, accordingly, the general purpose of business ethics is different: it is to oppose the self-interested practices of business in the name of morality, to try to get businesses generally to limit their profit seeking, to get businesses to distribute more altruistically whatever profits they do make, and to strengthen other social institutions capable of opposing the advance of business interests.

Business Ethics in the Context of the History of Ethics

In the context of the history of ethics, this is not surprising. Business ethics is an applied discipline, and one would expect it to apply the dominant ethical theories.

In Plato and to a lesser extent in Aristotle we read that practical concerns are low and vulgar. It follows that business, as an inherently practical enterprise, is hardly worthy of esteem. Given the place of Plato and Aristotle on the intellectual landscape, we have a partial explanation of the disdain that members of the cultural elite have always exhibited toward business.

In Immanuel Kant we read that there is an absolute duality of moral motivation (duty) and interest motivation (inclination): any hint of an interest destroys the moral worth of an action.[8] But since business is driven by interests, it follows that business is inherently amoral.

In John Stuart Mill we read that altruistic self-sacrifice for the collective is the standard of morality and that there is nothing worse than someone interested primarily in his own "miserable individuality."[9] But obviously business is driven by self-interest rather than altruism, individualism rather than collectivism, the profit motive rather than the motive of self-sacrifice; so business is immoral or amoral.

In Christianity and Marxism, we read the same moral themes: collectivism and human sacrifice. Christianity's core parable is Jesus' voluntarily undergoing crucifixion in order to cleanse humans of their sins. The parable illustrates (1) the necessity of human sacrifice: Jesus is strong and moral while the others are weak and immoral, and we solve the problems of the weak and immoral by sacrificing the strong and moral; and (2) collectivism: all humans get a share of Jesus' sacrifice whether they have earned it by their own efforts or not. (The same theme of collectivism is illustrated in the doctrine of Original Sin: responsibility is not individual; rather all humans bear the responsibility for Adam and Eve's actions.) Marxism's core slogan is "From each according to his ability, to each according to his need."[10] The slogan illustrates (1) the necessity of human sacrifice: some humans are strong and able while others are weak and needy, and we solve the problems of the weak and needy by sacrificing the strong and able; and (2) collectivism: each individual is seen as a collective asset, and his assets are redistributed to everyone whether they have earned it or not. For both Christianity and Marxism, self-interest and morality are opposed.

So it is not surprising that the discipline of business ethics today is simply applying to business what the dominant voices in the history of ethics have been saying for thousands of years.

This in turn explains why business ethicists tend not to be shy in calling for businesses to sacrifice their profits and why most business professionals are uneasy about the subject of business ethics. Business professionals are concerned with their self-interest, with making profits, and are well aware that most business ethicists, carrying the mantle of moral authority, either frown upon such things or put them in the category of lower priorities.

The duality of self-interest and morality is taken as a general and fundamental philosophical thesis in current business ethics, and it is as a general philosophical thesis that it must be addressed and, in my view, rejected. Defenders of business can and have expended great energy showing that particular self-interested business practices are both productive and win/win—the formation of limited corporations, the introduction of futures and "junk" bonds, and so on. But these particular demonstrations have done little to lessen general suspicion of about business.

An analogy to some brands of environmentalism is helpful here. For some environmentalists the beliefs that we are running out of resources and that industrial chemicals are poisoning everything function psychologically as general, axiomatic truths. Scientists and other experts can refute a particular fear—e.g., by showing that there is still plenty of oil and that Alar is benign—but the general thesis is left untouched: the environmentalist is still primed to expect the worst, and will continue to expect the worst even if the next dozen scares turn out to be groundless. Similarly, the general thesis that self-interest is outside of morality leads to a general suspicion of self-interest in business. So explaining, e.g., that some kinds of insider trading are not so bad after all is not going to change anyone's mind about the moral status of business: most ethicists will still be primed to expect the worst from the next manifestation of self-interest. It is the general thesis about self-interest that must be addressed.

So why have philosophers traditionally put morality and self-interest in different categories?

Self-Interest as Amoral/Immoral

Self-interest is argued to be a problem in business in two ways. First, the profit motive can lead one individual to harm another—that is, self-interest leads to sins of commission. For example, a standard argument about insider trading is that the insider is in a position to take unfair advantage of the outsider, and his self-interest leads him to do so. Second, the profit motive can lead individuals not to help the less fortunate—that is, self-interest leads to sins of omission. For example, the standard argument against plant relocations is not that the company is harming the rights of the workers; rather, since the workers will be in a more desperate situation, the moral company would be willing to give up the profit opportunities that a plant relocation would offer them.

The sins of commission worry is that self-interest puts individuals at odds with their obligations not to harm the interests of other individuals, and the sins of omission worry is that self-interest puts individuals at odds with their obligations to be altruistic. In both cases, morality is seen as requiring self-sacrifice. To avoid sins of commission I have to sacrifice an opportunity to gain, and to avoid sins of omission I have to sacrifice an asset. In both cases, conflicts of interests among individuals are taken to be fundamental. Let us take self-interest's two kinds of 'sins' separately.

Self-Interest and Sins of Commission

In greater detail, the sins of commission argument runs as follows:

We start by noting conflicts: business versus consumer (fraudulent advertising, monopolistic pricing); business versus employees (racist/sexist hiring, plant relocations); business versus other businesses (cut-throat pricing, insider trading).

We ask, What causes the conflicts? (a) Self-interest: in order to make a profit, the business is willing to cheat its customers, exploit its employees, do nasty things to competitors, harm the environment. (b) Relative weakness: consumers, workers, some competitors, the environment are not in a good position to defend themselves.

We next ask, What are the consequences of such conflicts? The stronger party prevails, and the weaker party loses.

We then generalize the problem: self-interest/the profit motive and the existence of inequalities of ability and power cause conflicts of interest and lead to the strong profiting at the expense of the weak.

Next we offer general ethical and political solutions: (a) Ethical: We require businesses to restrain their self-interest—i.e., to forego profit opportunities; (b) Political: We ask the government to regulate or impose restraints on business; and we ask the government to grant special rights to the weaker parties and/or limits the rights of the stronger parties.

So we get the negative solution: Business ethics is primarily about restraining self-interest and profit seeking.

The starting point of this analysis is also that there are fundamental conflicts of interest between businesses, consumers, and employees, and among businesses themselves. Once the conflicts are allowed as fundamental, one has to make a principled choice: Is one pro-business (and thereby anti-consumer and anti-labor), or pro-consumer and pro-labor (and thereby anti-business)?

The most important question here is: Why should we take conflicts of interest as fundamental? What is the source of this premise? If we are to say that a general and fundamental truth about morality is that self-interest should be sacrificed or set aside, then we must have as a premise that as a fundamental and general truth interests conflict. So the question is: Why are there seen to be general conflicts of interest?

Two global considerations about the human condition have traditionally been used to show that conflicts of interests are fundamental to the human condition. One is a premise about human psychology and biology; the other is a premise about economics.

Limited Resources

Let us take up first the economic premise: The claim that we live in a world of scarce resources. The concept of scarcity is used in a number of ways. A fairly neutral way is to say that humans always want more than they have. This is not the way in which it is used to attack self-interest. If the problem is simply that we want more, we can say that the solution then is to produce more.

But in traditional ethics, producing our way out of scarcity is not seen as an option. Scarcity is used in a Malthusian or zero-sum sense: there is not enough to go around. This puts us in conflict with each other: your need for food, for example, and my need for food cannot both be satisfied, so one of us has to sacrifice or be sacrificed. The problem then is deciding who it should be.

This is the reason for the popularity of lifeboat scenarios. Lifeboat scenarios illustrate what is often seen to be a fundamental economic fact that morality has to react to: That your self-interest and my self-interest are in fundamental conflict because of economic scarcity.

A lifeboat situation gives us a tough choice. The choice is either to act in stereotypically selfish fashion or to act altruistically. If I put my self-interest first, I will take whatever steps necessary to ensure that I get enough food and drink, thereby ensuring that someone else dies. I gain at the expense of someone else. If I put others first, I willingly sacrifice myself for the sake of someone else. Others gain at my expense. On the one hand, if everyone or anyone puts his self-interest first, a free for all battle will ensue, thus endangering the safety of the boat. On the other hand, an uncritical altruism might result in the only person with navigational skills throwing himself overboard, thus endangering the safety of the boat. Consequently, the argument runs, the reasonable thing is to adopt a collectivist standpoint—we should all put our self-interests aside and think what's best for the boat as a whole: whose needs are greatest, who has the most to contribute to the boat's survival?

What this implies for moral philosophy is that self-interest is dangerous. In a world of scarce resources self-interest leads to brutal competition, the harming of the weak by the strong, and the endangerment of society as a whole. What this implies for business is that profits must be made at the expense of others. In a world of scarce resources, business is fundamentally a zero-sum game: the profit motive leads to brutal competition, the exploiting of the weak by the strong, and the impoverishing of society as a whole.

According to this argument, then, conflicts of interest are necessary because of a fundamental economic truth: limited resources.

Gyges/Original Sin/the Id

The other major argument for fundamental conflicts of interest is grounded in claims about human psychology and biology. Consider the following quotations.

Here is Brian Medlin, author of a widely cited critique of ethical egoism: "[The egoist] can't even preach that he should look after himself and preach this alone. When he tries to convince me that he should look after himself, he is attempting so to dispose me that I shall approve when he drinks my beer and steals Tom's wife."[11] Here is Charles Sykes, a conservative intellectual: "The essence of naked egotism is imposing one's likes and dislikes and the subtle prejudices and whining annoyances of the self on others. Society exists to put limits on the desire of the ego to make itself the center of the universe."[12] Here is a quotation from Anthony Burgess, a well-known contemporary British novelist:

> That the sadomasochistic impulse is in all of us we no longer doubt. There is some obscure neural liaison in the brain between the sexual urge and the desire for domination—and the latter phrase I have deliberately left ambiguous. We are, quite rightly, scared of letting the sadomasochistic get out of hand: it is all too easy. We're all pretty bad inside; it's what we do outside that counts.[13]

What we have here are claims of what is thought to be the raw material, the basic human nature, that ethics has to deal with. We are by nature beings that want to steal from each other. We want to make cuckolds of each other. We are prejudiced and whiny and overbearing. And, if we are honest, we will admit that we get sexual pleasure out of beating and humiliating each other.

This has been a dominant theme in the history of arguments against self-interest. Most major philosophical opponents of self-interest have also advocated a grim picture of human nature. The moral of the Myth of Gyges, argues Plato, is that all people have in-built vulgar and unruly appetites that only a few, after long effort, will be able to subdue. Christianity's basic thesis is Original Sin: we are all born destructive, rebellious, we all have the mark of Cain the murderer on us. Sigmund Freud's concept of the id is of an irrational and nearly uncontrollable set of instincts that lead us to want to abuse our neighbor—or, in his own words, "to exploit his capacity for work without compensation, to use him sexually without his consent, to seize his possessions, to humiliate him, to cause him pain, to torture and kill him. *Homo homini lupus.*"[14]

Claims such as these go to the heart of the project of ethics. If these claims about human nature are true, then each individual is fundamentally in conflict with each other. We then have only two choices. We can be self-interested and let our animal natures run wild. But if we do, then obviously life will be nasty, solitary, brutish, and short, and civil society will collapse. The alternative is to attempt to make civil society possible. This project will require an anti-self-interest force— namely, a moral code that places priority on taming the self, on getting the self to suppress its in-built interests. Since human nature does not change over time, this project will also have to be an ongoing one: Ethics will always have to mean resolving fundamental conflicts of interest, and its solution will always be the sacrifice or restraint of self-interest.

Applied to business, we get the principle that antagonism and dominance, rather than cooperation and mutual benefit, are more natural to individuals. Short-term desires—for quick profits or expressions of power—will be a constant temptation. We get, for example, the view of business advocated by marketing professional Roger Dawson: "When you destroy the guy across the table, that's negotiating. When you make him thank you for it, that's power."[15]

In order that cooperation and long-term relationships can exist, the fundamental thesis of business ethics will be the suppression of self-interest. Business ethics will have to be eternally vigilant in the search for ways to thwart self-interest's desires to slip its restraints.

We now have two arguments that support the conclusion that conflicts of interest are fundamental. The argument about limited resources is heard more often from leftists, in keeping with their emphasis on nurture over nature factors, and the argument about destructive human nature is heard more often from conservatives, in keeping with their traditional emphasis on nature over nurture factors. Common to both, though is the conflict of interest conclusion and the consequent conclusions that self-interest is in need of restraint and that ethics is the tool of restraint. For both, in other words, morality and self-interest are in fundamentally different and opposed categories.

Self-Interest and Sins of Omission

We find the same conflict-of-interest conclusion when we consider the sins of omission argument against self-interest. The argument runs as follows:

- In life some individuals are able to support themselves and some are not.
- If the able do not give charity to the unable, the unable will suffer or die.
- But the self-interest of the able is not to sacrifice for the needs of the unable.
- Therefore, the interests of the able are in conflict with the interests of the unable.
- Altruism's premise: The interests of the unable are more important than the interests of the able.

- Therefore, the able should sacrifice what is necessary to satisfy the needs of the unable.
- Therefore, self-interest is immoral (via the 6th and 3rd lines of the argument).

The starting point of this analysis is that the interests of the unable put them in conflict with the interests of the able. If we think of this conflict as fundamental, then we have to make a principled choice: Since only one set of interests can be satisfied, we have to decide whether, in general, to sacrifice the interests of the able (as altruists do) or those of the unable (as, for example, Friedrich Nietzsche and Social Darwinists do). Requiring sacrifice from the able to help the unable is unpleasant, but not as harsh as not requiring that sacrifice seems. So we get the altruist conclusion: The needs of the unable should take precedence, and since the self-interest of the able is opposed to this, self-interest must be sacrificed.

Again it is a premise about conflicts of interest that is crucial here, this time by taking human inability as a fundamental that ethics has to respond to. If we take need and inability as fundamental for ethics, then conflicts of interest are inescapable and someone must be sacrificed. Altruism sides with those in greater need and thus rejects the self-interest of the able.

Applied to business ethics, we get the general conclusion that business ethics is partly about getting businesses to sacrifice their self-interest to the interests of the less able. Such altruism leads to (a) urging businesses to redistribute their profits to parties with greater need, and (b) support for government redistribution of wealth (e.g., by taxation, rent control, minimum wages).

Summarize: Why Conflicts of Interest?

Three considerations, then, lead to the conclusion that conflicts of interest are fundamental. In each case, sacrifice of self-interest is argued as an ethical fundamental: either the self is required to restrain itself or it is required to give away some of its assets.

If we take these background theses from ethical theory as general truths, we will turn to the applied field of business ethics with the two following assumptions in place:

1. Business is about making profits. But we suspect ahead of time that profits are made at the expense of others: business is generally win/lose.
2. So business is immoral to the extent that it is profitable.

Business is not altruistic in intent, i.e., business is not lose/win. But we know ahead of time that one is supposed to be altruistic or at least that one gets moral credit only for altruistic acts. So business is amoral or immoral.

Consequences of the Dualism: Target Inequalities

In all most traditional ethical theories, self-interest is the target of morality, but it is the self-interest of the better off, stronger, more able, richer parties that is specially targeted. The stronger party is in a better position to take advantage of the weaker, so it is the stronger party's self-interest that is in special need of restraint. It is the stronger party that should be sacrificing to help the weaker party, so it is the stronger party's self-interest that must be overcome. In both cases, inequalities of power, ability and wealth come to have enormous moral significance, and great inequalities polarize the moral obligations and claims of the strong and the weak. Those who are stronger are in special need of restraint and have greater obligations to redistribute their resources to the weaker. By contrast, those who are weaker are seen as especially deserving of extra rights against harm by the strong, and the greater their degree of weakness the greater their claims against the strong.

Consequently, in most current business ethics, analysis of business dealings takes as its starting point the relative degrees of strength of the involved parties. For example, consider the following examples of alleged sins of omission:

- Large corporations, seeking to increase their profits, will relocate their factories, leaving many individuals unemployed. Analysis: the corporation is "stronger" and the many individual employees are "weaker." Solution: The corporation should not relocate, thus sacrificing profit opportunities but benefiting the employees.
- Banks, acting in their self-interest, do not make loans to needy individuals in inner cities, and they foreclose on unpaid mortgages of, for example, unemployed individuals. Analysis: Banks are rich; inner city residents and unemployed people are poor. Solution: The banks should sacrifice for the poor by giving them high-risk loans.
- Self-interest leads some companies not to pay unskilled labor more than subsistence wages. Analysis: Owners of companies are financially stronger than their unskilled employees. Solution: The owners should sacrifice some profits for the employees.
- Maternity leave: corporations will be uncaring of the needs of their pregnant woman employees. Analysis: Corporations are stronger; pregnant women have special needs. Solution: The women should be given a guarantee of a position once maternity leave is over.

In each case, the analysis identifies a stronger and a weaker party and then requires a sacrifice by the stronger party to benefit the weaker party. The same procedure is followed for alleged sins of commission:

- Airwaves and the American government's Federal Communication Commission's traditional "Fairness

Doctrine": If unregulated, big radio corporations (strong) will manipulate the (weak) public's political views by presenting slanted coverage. Solution: The F.C.C. should regulate the content of broadcast media to ensure balanced coverage.

- Experimental medical drugs (e.g., Laetrile): To make a profit, pharmaceutical companies (strong) will exploit the fears and desperation of terminally ill patients (weak). Solution: The governmental Federal Trade Commission and/or the Food and Drug Administration should control the marketing of experimental drugs.

- Infant formula: Big western corporations (strong) will take advantage of poor, illiterate, third-world mothers (weak). Solution: Put pressure on the selling companies to limit sales, not to advertise, etc.

- Advertising of risky products (e.g., of tobacco, alcohol): Large companies (strong) will manipulate (weak) consumers' values and tastes through advertising. Solutions: regulate or eliminate such advertising; or use the business's property against its will for public interest messages (e.g., Canadian cigarette packaging).

- Apartment rentals: Rich landlords (strong) will gouge tenants (weak); Solution: Impose rent control to help the needy tenant at the expense of rich landlord.

- Insider trading: Wall Street investors (strong) will take advantage of the little guy investing from Main Street (weak). Solutions: Restrain insider trading; help the little guy by redistributing the big guy's information (e.g., disclosure laws).

- Wages: Employers (strong) will exploit employees (weak) by paying them only subsistence wages. Solution: Set a minimum wage to help the needy employee at the expense of the rich employer.

- Hiring policies: Businesses (strong) will act as racists and exists with respect to potential employees (weak). Solution: Establish affirmative action policies help members of less-well-off groups at the expense of members of better-off groups.
- Product safety: McDonald's Corporation (strong) will carelessly sell hot coffee to little old ladies (weak) in cars that don't even have a safe place to put a cup. Solution: Enforce strict liability.[16]

In each case, we identify a stronger and a weaker party. We take the interests of the two parties to be in fundamental conflict. We then propose solutions that at least restrain the self-interest of the stronger party in the name of protecting the weaker party, and in some cases actively sacrifice the interests of the stronger party to benefit the weaker. Since in relation to consumers, businesses are perceived as the stronger party, business ethics today focuses on giving consumers extra protections and limiting the powers of businesses. Since in relation to employees, employers are perceived as the stronger party, business ethics today focuses on giving employees special protections and limiting the powers of employers. Since in relation to small business, big business is perceived as stronger, business ethics focuses on giving small business a boost and on taming the dreaded multinational corporation.

We thus get a business ethic that sounds like the following: The moral big corporation will give much of its profits to charity; it will restrict its profit-making opportunities in poor third world countries; when advertising it will be less persuasive with respect to the helpless consumer; in order to give the little guy a chance to compete it won't use its size advantage; when employing, it will sacrifice some profitability if its employees need it. And if businesses won't sacrifice their interests voluntarily, then we'll ask the government to force them to. The government will see its job as helping the weak against the strong by giving them extra rights, limiting the rights of the strong, or transferring wealth from the strong to the weak.

Current business ethics thus bases itself on and fosters a general adversarial culture: business versus consumer, employer versus employee, big business versus small business, and business versus government.

It is against this sort of ethic that defenders of free enterprise have argued. However, they have generally not done so by attacking the ethic directly but rather by showing the impractical political and economic consequences of interfering with free markets.

Libertarians and some conservatives have argued, often well, that the proposed solutions in the above cases undermine incentive, violate individuals' liberties and property rights, violate the principle of equal rights, and so on. This, however, has had little effect on moral opposition to free enterprise—since most of those concerned with ethics have held that practical concerns are less significant than moral concerns, that the interest individuals have in their property and their incentive to acquire more are merely self-interests, and that such self- interested concerns can and should be limited, restrained, and overridden.

As long as self-interest is seen as amoral or immoral, arguing the practicality of the profit motive and property rights will have limited success. One's opponents may come to agree that free markets are efficient, but they will still be willing to sacrifice individual liberties and profits—those are merely self- interested considerations, after all—in the name of higher, moral considerations.

What is needed, then, is a defense of individualism, self-interest, on moral grounds. Until we have such a defense, calls for self-sacrifice—either voluntary or enforced politically—will be the norm in business ethics and in regulatory policy.

I have argued that opposition to self-interest stems from taking conflicts of interest to be fundamental to ethics, and that this stems from pessimistic economic, psychological, and biological premises. These premises make self-interest seem incompatible with long-term human survival. It is those economic and psychological theories that we need to address.

Here I turn to Ayn Rand's alternative. Rand has not often had a positive reception from the ethics community for a number of reasons. The major one is that she championed self- interest loudly and forcefully. For an ethics community com- mitted to the view that morality means restraining and sacrificing self-interest this could mean only one thing: She must be urging the strong to do whatever they feel like to the weak. That view, given the long history of ethics, could simply be rejected out of hand.

But such a rejection evaluates Rand's advocacy of self-interest from within a set of premises about economics and human nature that she rejects. She rejects the belief that ethics starts by taking conflicts of interest as fundamental. She rejects the view that ethics starts by reacting to scarce resources; she rejects the view that ethics starts by reacting to the nasty things some people want to do to each other; and she rejects the view that ethics starts by asking what to do about the poor and unable.

It is a philosopher's starting points that matter most. So what are Rand's?

Ayn Rand's Ethics

According to Rand, ethics is based on the requirements of life. That which makes life possible sets the standard of good; that which undermines or destroys life is the bad. Ethics is thus rooted in biology: the fact that life is conditional. The values needed for life are not automatically achieved, and since they are not automatically achieved, each human faces a fundamental alternative: to achieve the values necessary for life, or not. Achieving the values sustains one's life; not doing so leads to death. But the achieving of the values has preconditions. Each of us has to learn what values are necessary for life and what actions are necessary to achieve them, and then choose consistently to initiate those actions. But the learning of these things depends on a personal choice to think.[17]

In summary form, the points here are:

- Life requires the consumption of values.
- The values to be consumed must be produced.
- The production of values requires that we act in certain ways.
- Acting in those ways requires that we have the knowledge of what values we need to consume and what actions will produce them.
- Having the knowledge requires that we think and learn.

Or, in brief:

- Life depends on values.
- Values depend on production.
- Production depends on knowledge.
- Knowledge depends on thinking.[18]

The key thing about each of these points is that they are and can be performed only by individuals. Individualism is built into the nature of human life.

Start with the thinking requirement. Only an individual mind can think, and only an individual can initiate the thinking process. Others can help us enormously in our thinking process by providing us with information, guiding us from step to step, pointing out pitfalls—but others can only help. As much as they help, each of us is the only one who can do our thinking for us. Thinking is an individual process.

The result of good thinking—knowledge—resides in individual minds, and it can be put to productive use only by the initiative of an individual. Only individuals know things, and only individuals can put their knowledge into practice. Several individuals may have the same item of knowledge in their minds, or several individuals may decide to work cooperatively on a project that utilizes their different items of knowledge. But the initiation of the group project requires sustained initiative by the individuals involved. Groups don't do things; the individuals in the group do.

The result of productive action is some value to be consumed, used, enjoyed. Here again, the individual is the unit of reality. Only individuals are consumers. Only individuals can eat a salad, enjoy a friendship, or experience art. Two individuals may share a salad or a friendship, but the benefits are felt individually. A thousand individuals may hear the same symphony performance, but it is a thousand individual experiences.

In summary, the case for individualism is that only individuals think, only individuals know, only individuals act, and only individuals can consume the product of their actions. In other words, human life is individual. Individuals are both the producers of value and the consumers of value. Individuals are both the means of value seeking and the end of that value seeking. Others may assist or interfere in the process, but they cannot live your life for you.

These are the premises upon which egoism depends. The ethics of self-interest is based on the fact that human life is an individual phenomenon, that its maintenance is an individual responsibility in three fundamental ways: individuals must think, they must apply the results of their thinking productively, and they must consume the results of their productive actions. It is thus the needs of the rational, productive individual that are fundamental in Rand's ethics.

Elements of this view have been noted by other philosophers, economists and biologists. But they have never been recognized as fundamentally significant for ethics. That is because other facts (or alleged facts) have been given priority, and to the extent those other facts were given priority the requirements of the rational, self-interested producer were subordinated. Those alleged facts were the conclusion that conflicts of interest are fundamental, and the premises that resources are scarce, that human nature is destructive, and that the needs of the unable are prior.

Let us see how Rand's claims of fundamentality compare to these other claims.

Responding to Limited Resources

Take the problem of scarce resources or lifeboat economics. Zero-sum economics is a problem of production. If we subsisted as other animals do, as hunters and gatherers of a limited supply, then our economic predicament would indeed be essentially zero-sum.

But by the application of reason humans are capable of increasing net production. If we have reason, then science is possible, and with it engineering and technology. In other words, reason makes possible production—and not merely hunting and gathering. And if production is possible, then economics is not the science of life on a lifeboat.

Thus, taking scarce resources as a fundamental fact about human life is simply false. Resources are not limited in the sense required to generate conflicts of self-interest. I am not in conflict with you for a limited supply of goods, for by thinking and producing I can increase the supply of goods. The increase is not made at another's expense. If I am a scientist who creates a better hybrid of corn, I increase the net stock of food. If I am an inventor who improves the efficiency of a loom, I increase the net stock of cloth.

Whatever my profession, it is to my self-interest to think and produce, as it is to everyone's self-interest. There is a fundamental harmony of self-interest here, rather than a conflict—others' reasoning and producing increases the supply of goods, as does mine, making it possible for us to trade to mutual advantage.[19]

(It is an important historical point that most major ethical philosophies were formed before the rise of science and before the Industrial Revolution transformed human productive ability. There was, accordingly, a lesser grasp of power of reason and the possibilities of production. To the extent production was not seen as an option, the focus shifted to the zero-sum game of distribution.)

Responding to Gyges/Original Sin/Id

Now let us turn to the traditional claim that conflicts of interest are fundamental because we are born with other-destructive desires. This claim depends on saying that our desires are primaries, that our characters are formed by forces largely beyond our control, that reason has no fundamental role in determining our values and hence our emotions. If it is true that emotion is prior to and more powerful than reason, then conflicts among individuals are necessary and self-restraint is necessary. If, on the other hand, emotions are consequent to reason, then conflict is not necessary.

Rand argues that individuals are born cognitively, emotionally, and morally *tabula rasa*, that reason is primary in shaping one's values, and that emotions are consequences of one's value choices. This means one is not born preset with destructive values, which means that it is possible to shape one's value system and character. This in turn means that the achieving of a great character, rather than the suppressing of a bad character, is our fundamental ethical project: Ethics is about self- development rather than self-restraint. If so, there are no inherent conflicts among men on this basis. Self-interest is not the enemy of ethics if individuals are capable of directing their lives by reference to their long-term rational interests.

We have here only two opposed sets of assertions—the traditionalists' and Rand's—and a huge set of nativism and *tabula rasa* issues would need to be addressed before deciding one way or the other. Let me focus only on one more limited issue. Whether emotions are acquired or innate, it is nonetheless true that many individuals have other-destructive drives and the habit of short-range thinking. Even if one agrees that in the long-term a commitment to rationality and productiveness is the standard of good, opportunities do present themselves in which one can make a short-term gain at the expense of someone else and get away with it.

For example, suppose you are normally a productive individual, but you have an opportunity to steal $1 million and get away with it. Why not?

Rand's general solution is clear: The ethical fundamental is that life requires production. And so a principled commitment to production is the moral core. Production requires knowledge, facing facts, integrity. In a social context, production and trade require cooperation, which requires honesty, justice, respect for property rights, abiding by agreements, and so on. Thieves are parasitic upon this process: they do not produce, nor do they help the process of production. They do not trade, nor do they facilitate trade. Thieves undercut the system of production and trade: they harm those who make production and trade possible. So thievery is ruled out on principle.

But the particular question comes back: Why stick by the long-term commitment to production if a short-term commitment to thievery will yield you more?

The issue is being able to separate the short-term parasitism from the rest of one's life. One's life is a long-term commitment, and it requires a set of long-term principles to guide it and give it meaning. Who one is and what one achieves depends on one's long-term commitments. A thief, by contrast, thinks short-range: I can get away with it. Maybe he can, and maybe he can't. That is not the primary issue.

Consider an analogy to marriage. A marriage is successful if both parties share a deep mutuality of interests and both are committed to a long-term development of those interests. Suppose the husband in such a relationship is away on a business trip and is offered a prostitute for the evening. He knows his wife is not likely to find out, and he can practice safe sex so there's not much chance of catching syphilis. Is it to his self-interest to go for it? If he is committed to the marriage, then clearly not: Sleeping with a prostitute destroys the integrity of the marriage. But if he is not committed to the marriage, then he will miss out on all that such relationships can offer. In either case, his long-term self-interest is not achieved.

Returning to the temptation to thievery. One's life and its meaning are deeper and more long-term than marriage and the principles that inform it need to be as deeply held. Injecting parasitism into one's life is like injecting a prostitute into one's marriage.

The solution to the problem of short-run temptations is to promote the long-term. This requires rational identification of one's long-term interest and the principles of action necessary to achieve it. This is what ethics should be about.

This is not what the conflict model of morality offers as a solution to the problem of thieves. Thieves are motivated by the desire for gain, so the traditional morality condemns the desire for gain as such. Taking the view that individuals are short-run and passion-driven, the only solution possible to it is to teach restraint. Rather than saying that the desire for gain is healthy and moral, but that there are proper and improper ways to gain, it condemns the only thing that makes life possible.

Consider teaching ethics to your child. Suppose that your child steals, whines to get his way, or hits another child to get something. The child is "selfish": he believes that stealing, whining, and hitting are practical means to his ends. The traditional restraint model teaches him: Yes, those are practical means to your ends, but you must either renounce your ends or the means for the sake of others. By contrast, the rational egoist model teaches him: No, those are not practical means to your ends; rather, productiveness, friendliness, and cooperation are practical means to your ends. The difference is crucial. It is the difference between teaching the child that self-fulfillment is immoral because it means stepping on others and teaching him that self-fulfillment is a worthy goal and there is a rational, non-conflicting way to achieve it.

Responding to the Needs of the Unable

Solving the problems of the unable is given less emphasis in the current business ethics literature. The recent emphasis is more on preventing sins of commission than on promoting charity. When the promotion of charity or compulsory redistribution does appear in the literature, the argument is that (a) the interests of the unable take precedence over those of the able, (b) that the responsibility for solving unable's problems lies primarily with the able, (c) that giving to charity is a sacrifice of self-interest, but (d) that the able should see their assets as belonging to all who have need of them.

From what has been said above, it is clear that Rand's ethics rejects all of the above. She rejects the collectivist premise: Individuals are not primarily means to the ends of others. Further, since the unable depend on the able, the needs of the able take precedence: the requirements of production take precedence over the requirements of distribution. And charity for the temporarily unfortunate is not necessarily against one's self-interest. If my charity can help someone get back on his feet and become self-supporting, I benefit: the more rational producers there are in the world, the better off I am. Most individuals are capable of exercising self-responsibility and supporting themselves. Charity becomes a minor issue in ethics: It becomes a matter of good will rather than duty—a matter of individuals who can afford it helping those who deserve it out of a difficult situation.[20]

The problem of the unable only creates a fundamental conflict with the interests of the able if there is no long-term solution to the problems of the unable. But for most of the reasons why individuals become unable to support themselves, long-term solutions are possible. If the problem is limited resources, science and production are solutions. Accidents of nature such as earthquakes and floods can be addressed and recovered from fairly quickly. Poverty caused by repressive politics can be solved politically: bad politics is not a law of nature. Inability due to personal laziness or bad judgment is correctable. This leaves the small minority of individuals who are severely handicapped either physically or mentally; for these individuals the only option is charity from the able. But again, the able do not exist to serve the unable: charity is an act of goodwill, not duty.[21]

Conclusion

The heart of Rand's strategy is to make fundamental the role of reason in human life. Reason makes possible science and production, long-term planning, and living by principle. It is these that make individuals flourish, and it is these that eliminate the idea that there are fundamental conflicts of interests among individuals.

Business is then one application. In business the moral individual is the producer: the individual who is an end in himself, independent in thought and action. Moral social relations are voluntary interactions to mutual benefit by productive individuals. Businesses and consumers, employers and employees are self-responsible ends in themselves who trade to mutual advantage. Neither is fundamentally in conflict with another, and neither is to be sacrificed to the other. Given these broad non-conflicting principles, differences over details are sorted out by negotiation. Governments enforce the non-conflicting principles and protect the negotiated contracts.

Objectivism's defenders of business claim three things:

- that the standard of value is one's self-interest,
- that the purpose of business is to achieve a profit,
- that the purpose of government is to protect individuals' rights to their lives, liberties, and property.

No, they are not, say their critics. In writing about ethics they say self-interest is dangerous to others—and besides, individuals should be selflessly serving the interests of others. In writing about business they say the profit motive is a dangerous, other-destructive force—and besides, a business should see itself as a servant of society as a whole. In writing about politics they say a laissez-faire policy leaves individuals too much freedom to do damage to each other—and besides, the purpose of government is to redistribute society's assets in the collective interest.

It is the anti-self-interest ethic that has been the major source of opposition to business and the free society. This I think explains the rather modest success of the strategy of explaining patiently how free markets and the profit motive lead to practical success and how socialism leads to practical failure. All of these have been demonstrated in theory and practice for 200 years but have had little effect on the opposition: pointing out the practical success of self-interest and the profit motive will not much affect those who put morality in a different, more important category

Only a moral defense of self-interest, combined with an understanding of free market economics and classical liberal politics, will advance the free society and business, its economic engine.

Some libertarians and conservatives have done well in promoting the economics and politics. But we need Ayn Rand for the ethics.

References

1. Michalos, Alex. *The Society for Business Ethics Newsletter* 5:1 (May 1994); p.6.
2. Dennis P. Quinn and Thomas M. Jones. "An Agent Morality View of Business Policy." *Academy of Management Review* 20:1 (1995), 22–42; p.22.
3. Sen, Amartya. *On Ethics and Economics*. New York: Basil Blackwell, 1987; p.15.
4. Gini, Al. "Speaking with Al Gini." Interview published in *Prentice-Hall Publishing Catalogue*, 1995–1996.
5. Bowie, Norman. "Challenging the Egoistic Paradigm." *Business Ethics Quarterly* 1:1 (1991), 1–21; pp. 11–12.
6. Oliver F. Williams, Frank K. Reilly, & John W. Houck. *Ethics & the Investment Industry*, eds. 1989. Rowman & Littlefield; p. 9.
7. William Shaw and Vincent Barry. *Moral Issues in Business*. 5th ed. Wadsworth, 1994; p. 16.
8. Kant, Immanuel. *Groundwork of the Metaphysic of Morals*. Translated by H.J. Paton. Harper Torchbooks, 1964; pp. 397–298.
9. Mill, John Stuart. *Utilitarianism*. Hackett Publishing; p. 14. See also p. 11 and pp. 14–16 where Mill repeatedly emphasizes that Utilitarian standard is not self-interest but the collective interest, to which the individual should be willing to sacrifice his life and happiness.
10. Marx, Karl. *Critique of the Gotha Program*. 1875.
11. Medlin, Brain. "Ultimate Principles and Ethical Egoism." *Australian Journal of Philosophy* 35:2 (1957), pp. 111–118.
12. Sykes, Charles. "The Ideology of Sensitivity." *Imprimis* 21 (July 1992), p. 4.
13. Burgess, Anthony. "Our Bedfellow, the Marquis de Sade." In *The Norton Reader*, 6th ed., p. 510.

14. Freud, Sigmund. *Civilization and Its Discontents*. W. W. Norton & Co., 1961; p. 58. Latin translation: "Man is a wolf to man."

15. Dawson, Roger. From promotional materials for Nightingale–Conant Corporation, 1994.

16. In 1992, an elderly woman purchased coffee from a McDonald's restaurant drive-through window. She then placed the hot coffee between her legs and attempted to open the lid. The coffee spilled on her lap; she was injured as a result and she sued McDonald's Corporation for not warning her that the coffee was hot. This case made the national press because she won a multi-million dollar settlement from McDonald's (the settlement was later reduced to less than a million dollars).

17. Rand, Ayn. "The Objectivist Ethics." In *The Virtue of Selfishness*. New York: New American Library, 1964; pp. 15–23.

18. "Man's mind is his basic tool of survival. Life is given to him, survival is not. His body is given to him, its sustenance is not. To remain alive, he must act, and before he can act he must know the nature and purpose of his action. He cannot obtain his food without a knowledge of food and of the way to obtain it. He cannot dig a ditch—or build a cyclotron—without a knowledge of the aim and the means to achieve it. To remain alive, he must think." (Ayn Rand, *Atlas Shrugged*. Random House, 1957; p. 1012)

19. See also Ludwig von Mises: "The natural scarcity of the means of sustenance forces every living being to look upon all other living beings as deadly foes in the struggle for survival, and generates pitiless biological competition. But with man these irreconcilable conflicts of interests disappear when, and as far as, the division of labor is substituted for economic autarky of individuals,

families, tribes, and nations. Within the system of society there is no conflict of interests as long as the optimum size of population has not been reached. As long as the employment of additional hands results in a more than proportionate increase in the returns, harmony of interests is substituted for conflict People are no longer rivals in the struggle for the allocation of portions out of a strictly limited supply. They become cooperators in striving after ends common to all of them. An increase in population figures does not curtail, but rather augments, the average shares of the individuals." (*Human Action*, 3rd revised edition, p. 667)

20. Rand, Ayn. "The Ethics of Emergencies." *The Virtue of Selfishness.* New York: New American Library, 1964.

21. Also, if one genuinely cares about helping the poor, then one will be a forceful advocate of the only economic system that has proved capable of generating the economic surplus that the poor depend upon.

This essay is based on a lecture given to the Ayn Rand Society at the American Philosophical Association, New York, NY, December 29, 1995. It was first published in the *Journal of Accounting, Ethics & Public Policy* 3:1 (Winter 2003), pp. 1-26.

Stephen R. C. Hicks is Professor of Philosophy at Rockford University, Illinois, USA, Executive Director of the Center for Ethics and Entrepreneurship, and Senior Scholar at The Atlas Society.

He received his B.A. and M.A. degrees from the University of Guelph, Canada, and his Ph.D. from Indiana University. His publications include *Explaining Postmodernism: Skepticism and Socialism from Rousseau to Foucault* (Scholargy Publishing, 2004; Expanded Edition, 2011), *Nietzsche and the Nazis* (Ockham's Razor, 2010), *Readings for Logical Analysis* (co-edited with David Kelley, W. W. Norton & Co., 1994, second edition 1998), *Entrepreneurial Living* (co-edited with Jennifer Harrolle, CEEF, 2016), and essays and reviews in academic and other publications.

Dr. Hicks can be reached via his website, StephenHicks.org.

Our Work

Publications: From graphic novels to textbooks to pocket guides, our books are available in multiple formats and languages

Narrative Videos: From animation to comedic features, our productions include *Draw My Life* videos and graphic novel-style compilations

Educational Resources: Online courses, podcasts, webinars, campus speaking tours, living-history presentations, and campus activism projects are among the wealth of ways we educate students of all ages about reason, achievement, individualism, and freedom

Student Programs: Our Atlas Advocates are eager, curious, and thoughtful students who meet for monthly book club discussions, and Richard Salsman, Ph.D.'s Morals & Markets webinar course; Our Atlas Intellectuals are adults who meet monthly to bring Ayn Rand's philosophy to ear on current events and real-world topics, curated by Stephen Hicks, Ph.D.

Commentaries: In addition to educational resources, our website offers commentaries on a wide range of political, cultural, and personal topics and events.

The Atlas Society is a 501(c)(3) non-profit organization, supported exclusively by private donors.